# The Life Cycle of a

# RABBIT

## John Williams

Illustrated by
## Jackie Harland

Reading Consultant:
## Diana Bentley

**The Bookwright Press**
**New York · 1988**

# Life Cycles

First published in the
United States in 1988 by
The Bookwright Press
387 Park Avenue South
New York, NY 10016

First published in 1988 by
Wayland (Publishers) Limited
61 Western Road, Hove
East Sussex, BN3 1JD, England

ISBN 0-531-18189-8
Library of Congress Catalog Card Number 87-73162

Typeset in the UK by DP Press Limited, Sevenoaks, Kent
Printed by Casterman S.A., Belgium

**Notes for parents and teachers**
Each title in this series has been specially written and
designed as a first natural history book for young readers.
For less able readers there are introductory captions,
while the more detailed text explains each illustration.

# Contents

All the words that are
in **bold** are explained in
the glossary on page 31.

# A rabbit is a **mammal.**

What is a mammal? It is an animal that has warm blood and feeds on its mother's milk when it is young. Most mammals have hair to keep them warm. The young grow inside their mother's body before they are born. Rabbits, cats, dogs, horses and people are all mammals.

# What do rabbits eat?

Rabbits do not eat meat. They like to
eat grass, leafy plants and vegetables.
They will eat the lettuce in your garden
if they can! To help them, they have
special sharp cutting teeth.

# This female rabbit is pregnant.

Mother rabbits can have as many as nine babies at one time. They grow in a special part of her body called the **womb**. While she is waiting, the mother builds a nest for her babies from her own fur.

# The rabbits grow inside the mother's body.

Look at the picture on the right. These baby rabbits are shown growing inside their mother's womb. While they are inside their mother's body they are called **embryos**. Look at the drawing below. If you could see inside a rabbit, this is where you would find the womb.

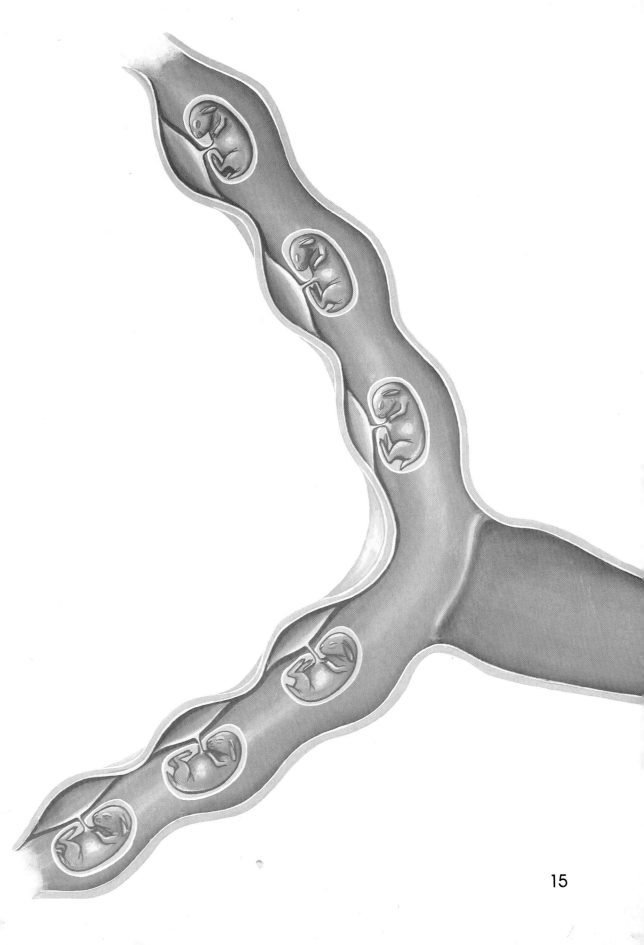

15

# A newborn litter of rabbits.

A group of newborn baby rabbits is called a litter. When they are born, the baby rabbits have no fur. They cannot see at first and need their mother to take care of them.

# The mother rabbit feeds her young.

Because the rabbits are helpless, the mother must protect them. She will keep them warm. She will feed her young with the milk that is made in her body for them.

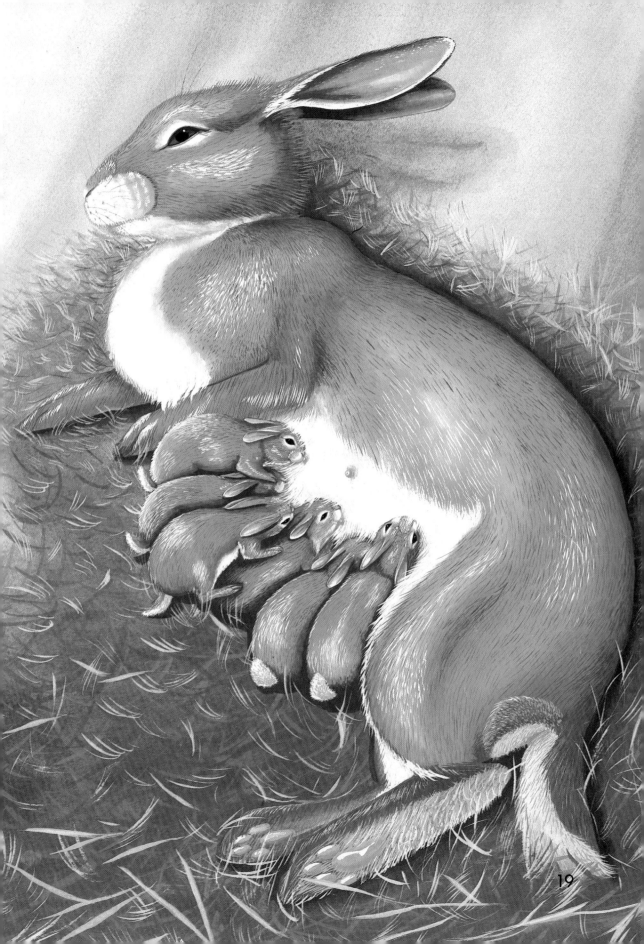

19

20

# The young come out of the burrow for the first time.

After a few weeks, the babies have grown fur. They are now big enough to come outside and explore. They begin to look for food. The mother still takes care of them, but the male rabbit will not do this.

# The young rabbits begin to use their teeth.

When the young rabbits are used to coming out of the burrow, their mother stops feeding them. Now they have to find their own food. They have grown sharp front teeth for cutting and have back teeth to grind leaves and grass so that they can easily swallow.

23

# Rabbits have many enemies.

Rabbits are hunted by other animals. They must take care not to be caught by them. **Weasels, stoats,** cats and some large birds will try to catch them. Rabbits use their noses, eyes and large ears to warn them of danger.

# The full-grown rabbits.

Rabbits like to eat and play in the evenings and early mornings. They also spend time **gnawing** at logs to keep their front teeth from growing too long. When they are about three months old, rabbits begin looking for a mate. They are ready to start new families.

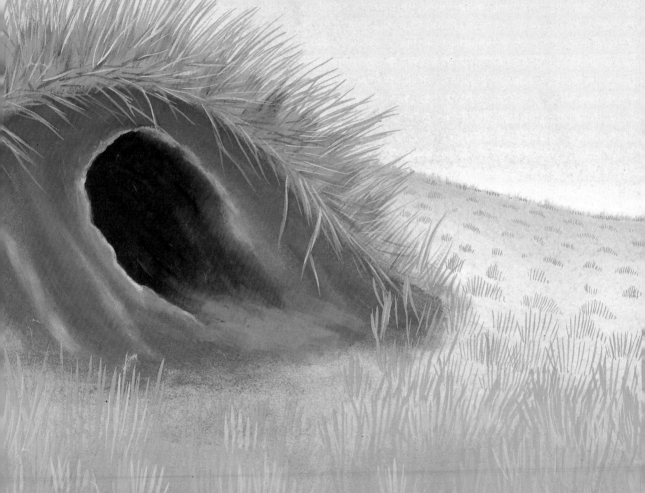

hutch

Old English rabbit

water bottle

wire fence

food bowl

straw bedding

# Take care of your pet rabbit.

Give your rabbit a large space in which
to move and play. It will need a lot of
fresh grass and leaves to eat each day.
It will need a warm, dry hutch to sleep
in. This will protect it from its enemies. If it
is a long-haired rabbit, it may need
combing and brushing. Hold it carefully.
Never hold it by its ears.

28

Old English
rabbit ►

◄ Angora
rabbit

Dutch
rabbit ►

29

# The life cycle of a rabbit.

How many stages of the life cycle of a rabbit can you remember?

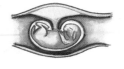

# Glossary

**Burrows**  Holes, dug by animals to live and shelter in.

**Embryos**  The name given to young animals before they are born.

**Gnawing**  When rabbits nibble at logs to keep their teeth from growing too long it is called **gnawing**.

**Mammals**  Warm-blooded animals that feed on their mothers' milk until their teeth grow.

**Mate**  This is when male (father) and female (mother) animals join together. It is how a baby animal is made.

**Pregnant**  When a female mammal has a baby growing inside her, she is **pregnant**.

**Sperm**  A liquid from the male which mixes with the eggs inside the female's body. If this does not happen, the eggs will not grow.

**Stoat**  An ermine, especially when in its brown summer coat. Stoats are members of the weasel family.

**Warren**  A group of tunnels and holes underground where many rabbits live together.

**Weasels**  Small, fierce mammals that live on small animals, birds' eggs, etc. They have a reddish-brown fur and long bodies with short legs.

**Womb**  The part of a female mammal's body where babies grow.

# Finding out more

Here are some books to read to find out more about rabbits.

*The Answer Book about Animals* by Mary Elting. Purnam, 1984.
*Discovering Rabbits and Hares* by Keith Porter. Franklin Watts, 1986.
*How Animals Behave* by Donald J. Crump, ed. National Geographic Society, 1984.
*How Animals Live* by Philip Steele. Franklin Watts, 1985.
*Rabbits: All About Them* by Alvin and Virginia Silverstein. Lothrop, 1973.
*Rabbits and Hares* by Colleen Bare. Dodd, 1983.

# Index